D0734676

Kipling

Victorian Balladeer

First published in Great Britain by Brockhampton Press,
a member of the Hodder Headline Group,
20 Bloomsbury Street, London WC1B 3QA

ISBN 1 86019 202 5

Created and produced by Flame Tree Publishing,
part of The Foundry Creative Media Company Limited,
The Long House, Antrobus Road, Chiswick, London W4 5HY

Special thanks to
Kate Brown and Kelley Doak for their work on this series

Printed and bound in U.A.E.

Kipling

Victorian Balladeer

Written and Compiled by
K. E. SULLIVAN

Contents

Introduction

'Kipling strikes me personally as the most complete man of genius (as distinct from fine intelligence) that I have ever known.'
Henry James

FROM THE last decades of the nineteenth century until well after the First World War, Rudyard Kipling was undoubtedly the most popular writer in the English language, and widely considered to be the greatest English poet and story-teller. Kipling was very much a narrator for his time, providing shrewd and engaging accounts of life in the barracks, in the homes and workplaces of the humble people of the British Empire. He wrote of life in Anglo-India, and in the strange country which surrounded it. His jungle stories, inspired by an Indian nurse he shared with his sister as a child, represent some of the most startlingly imaginative prose and verse undertaken by an English author.

He was also passionate about England, calling it 'the most wonderful foreign land I have ever been in', and describing its people, traditions and history in what has been considered the most vital impression of England's past, forming a succession of 'scents and sights and sounds' which reaches to the very heart of his adopted country. He took as his subjects political causes, commentaries on Industrialism and imperialism, engineering, technology, science and the military. He wrote as fluently for children as he did for the adults; his poems and prose cross the socio-economic divide, appealing almost unanimously. Because of this, Kipling was often described as lightweight, his accessibility, and lack of pretension mistaken for intellectual inferiority. T. S. Eliot wrote of Kipling, 'We expect a poet to be reproached for lack of respect for the intelligence of the common man, or even for deliberately flouting the intelligence of the common man ...

We expect a poet to be ridiculed because his verse does not appear to scan: we must defend Kipling against the charge of writing jingles. In short, people are exasperated by poetry which they do not understand, and contemptuous of poetry which they understand without effort ...'

Rudyard Kipling was born in Bombay on 30 December 1865, when India was very much a part of the British Empire. He was tended, with his sister Alice, by an Indian nurse, and he grew up in the traditional colonial style, where the exotic and primitive country outside his doors played little or no part in his life. When Kipling was six, he and Alice returned to England in order to be educated. They were left in the care of a retired naval officer and his wife, Captain and Mrs Holloway, at Southsea, and their parents returned to India. The next six years were tortuous for Kipling and his sister. Kipling was often forbidden books as punishment, and read in secret, causing damage to his eyes. Kipling later called this household, 'the house of desolation'.

In 1877, his mother returned from India, and he and Alice were taken to Devonshire where they spent the summer. He visited France with his father, which sparked in him a lifelong interest in that country and its people. In the autumn of 1877 he was sent to the United Services College at Westward Ho in Devonshire, to be educated by the army. It was here that he became deeply inspired to read and to write, and where his passionate love for England and her history was spawned. His years in Devonshire are chronicled in *Stalky & Co.*, some of the greatest schoolboy stories in existence. He read voraciously in French and in English, making up for his years of stifled learning.

When Kipling was seventeen, he joined his father, a principal at the Mayo School of Art, in Lahore, Northwest India. He took a reporting job on the *Civil and Military Gazette* in the Punjab, and for the next seven years learned about and grew to love the country of his birth. He developed a fascination for India, and he travelled a great deal, developing a perspective that was unusual for an English colonial. He began to write poems and short stories about the British soldier, including *Plain Tales from the Hills* (1888) and *Barrack-Room Ballads* (1892) which he printed himself. *The Light that Failed* (1890) established him as an author of note, but was followed by a nervous breakdown, the product of the stresses of earning a living as a writer.

In 1892, he married an American friend's sister, Caroline Balestier. Kipling and his new wife travelled across the world, although their trip was cut short by the collapse of the Oriental Banking Company in which Kipling had his savings. They settled in Vermont, where their first child Josephine was born, and where *Many Inventions*, and *The Jungle Books* were written.

Their second daughter, Elsie was born in 1896, and their son John the following year. They were visited often by Kipling's father, and Kipling continued to write prolifically, in between travelling extensively. In 1896 the Kiplings returned to England, where *Captains Courageous* was written in response to a memorial service for the men from the Gloucester fishing fleet, who had been lost or drowned in the year. In 1899, Kipling paid a visit to America, which resulted in a life-threatening attack of pneumonia and the death of Josephine, an event which caused the Kipling family considerable distress. They would not return to America.

Kipling and his family settled in Sussex, and it was here that he wrote *Kim*, a book which had been worked out in Kipling's mind for many years and which many consider to be the embodiment of his mature talents. Sussex life was a great inspiration to Kipling, and the purchase of a home near Sussex Downs, called Batemans, inspired a collection of historical fiction about Roman times in England entitled *Puck of Pook's Hill* and *Rewards and Fairies*. *Just So Stories*, *The Five Nations* and many other volumes were published throughout these years in Sussex, and in 1907 Kipling was awarded the Nobel Prize for Literature.

The First World War brought tragedy to the Kipling household, when John was killed fighting in France. Kipling withdrew into himself and his work, spending many hours producing prose and verse dedicated to the war effort. He wrote a number of war pamphlets, and in 1917 became a member of the Imperial War Graves Commission. In 1919, *Rudyard Kipling's Verse* was published, to enormous acclaim, but Kipling, distraught and unable to cope following the death of his son, spent increasingly long periods of time at his Sussex farmhouse. He continued to write, publishing *A Diversity of Creatures*, *The Years Between* and *Letters of Travel* over the next years, but his spirit was broken and his creative drive compromised by his situation, and he found little pleasure in his work.

His sparkling wit and ability to satirize have made him one of the most quoted authors of all time, with ever-recalled gems like 'And a woman is only a woman, but a good cigar is a Smoke,' and 'Oh, East is East, and West is West, and never the twain shall meet' tripping off tongues as often today as they did seventy years ago.

Kipling was largely responsible for the development of the short story, establishing it as a major genre well before it flourished in the hands of authors such as Joseph Conrad, E. M. Forster, D. H. Lawrence, and Somerset Maugham, and he wrote confidently on an enormous range of subjects, in which he related with sophistication and simplicity the issues of the day. His poetry is equally far-ranging, both interjected into his prose, and standing alone as major works of the late nineteenth and early twentieth centuries. He was inspired by the Pre-Raphaelite poets, and by Swinburne, and several of his poems echo Browning. Eliot called Kipling not a poet but a 'ballad writer', and it is clear that the story in Kipling's verse is far more central to its success than its structure and rhythm. He said, 'With this simplicity of purpose goes a consummate gift of word, phrase and rhythm. There is no poet who is less open to the charge of repeating himself.'

In 1935, a year before his death, Kipling began work on his autobiography, entitled *Something of Myself for My Friends Known and Unknown*, a strangely revealing work which has provided seemingly unlimited insight into the man and his creative process. He died on 18 January 1936, a month from the death of King George V, and he was buried in Westminster Abbey. His works have been continually in print since that day.

Author's Note

Kipling's verse encompasses an extraordinary range of themes and styles, some of it simplistic in its marching rhythm, some of it curiously ballad-like, and still more complicated and inventive. There is a distinct migration towards experimental verse in his later years, but Kipling's fluidity is never compromised. This selection represents work dating from his maturing style; his early work, what T.S. Eliot called 'juvenilia' and 'light reading in an English newspaper' has not been reproduced here. The poems that follow were chosen for their unique quality, for their diversity, for their unsurpassed ability to enlighten and to entertain.

Chronology

1865 Rudyard Kipling born in Bombay, 30 December.
1878 Kipling admitted to the United Services College at Westward Ho in Devon.
1881 Editor of the *United Services College Chronicle*. *Schoolboy Lyrics* privately printed by his parents.
1882 Finishes school and sails to India, works on *Military Gazette*.
1884 *Echoes* is published.
1885 *Quartette* is published.
1888 *Plain Tales from the Hills* is published.
1889 Travels across the Far East to America and then London.
1890 Suffers breakdown. *The Light that Failed* published.
1891 Visits South Africa, New Zealand and India. Returns to England. *Life's Handicap* published.

1892 Marries Caroline Starr Balestier, and settles in Vermont. Daughter Josephine born.
1893 *Many Inventions* published.
1894 *The Jungle Book* published.
1895 *The Second Jungle Book* published.
1896 Daughter Elsie born. Returns to England, settles in Sussex.
1897 Son, John born. *Captains Courageous* published.
1899 Josephine dies. Kipling seriously ill. *The Day's Work* published.
1901 *Kim* published.
1902 *Just So Stories* published.
1903–6 *The Five Nations, Traffics and Discoveries*, *Puck of Pook's Hill* published.
1907 Wins Nobel Prize for Literature. *Collected Verse* published.
1901-18 *Actions and Reactions*, *Abaft the Funnel*, *Rewards and Fairies*, *Songs from Books*, and war pamphlets published.
1915 John reported missing; never found.
1917 Kipling is made member of the Imperial War Graves Commission.
1919–33 *A Diversity of Creatures*, *The Years Between*, *Rudyard Kipling's Verse: Inclusive Edition*, *Letters of Travel*, *The Irish Guards in the Great War*, *Land and Sea Tales for Scouts and Guides*, *Debits and Credits*, *A Book of Words*, *Thy Servant a Dog*, *Limits and Renewals*, *Souvenirs of France* all published.
1927 Travels to Brazil.
1936 Kipling dies, 18 January.
1937 *Something of Myself for My Friends Known and Unknown* published.

The Ballad of East and West

EXTRACT

OH, EAST is East, and West is West, and never
the twain shall meet,
Till Earth and Sky stand presently at God's
great Judgment Seat;
But there is neither East nor West, Border, nor
Breed, nor Birth,
When two strong men stand face to face, though
they come from the ends of the earth!

Kamal is out with twenty men to raise
the Border-side,
And he has lifted the Colonel's mare that is
the Colonel's pride.
He has lifted her out of the stable-door between
the dawn and the day,
And turned the calkins upon her feet, and
ridden her far away.
Then up and spoke the Colonel's son that led
a troop of the Guides:
'Is there a never a man of all my men can
say where Kamal hides?'

L'Envoi

(*DEPARTMENTAL DITTIES*)

THE SMOKE upon your Altar dies,
The flowers decay,
The Goddess of your sacrifice
Has flown away.
What profit then to sing or slay
The sacrifice from day to day?

'We know the Shrine is void,' they said,
'The Goddess flown –
'Yet wreaths are on the altar laid –
'The Altar-Stone
'Is black with fumes of sacrifice,
'Albeit She has fled our eyes.

'For, it may be, if still we sing
'And tend the Shrine,
'Some Deity on wandering wing
'May there incline;
'And, finding all in order meet,
'Stay while we worship at Her Feet.'

When Earth's Last Picture is Painted, 1892

(L'ENVOI TO 'THE SEVEN SEAS')

WHEN EARTH'S last picture is painted and the tubes
are twisted and dried,
When the oldest colours have faded, and the
youngest critic has died,
We shall rest, and, faith, we shall need it – lie down
for an æon or two,
Till the Master of All God Workmen shall put us
to work anew.

And those that were good shall be happy: they shall sit
in a golden chair;
They shall splash at a ten-league canvas with
brushes of comets' hair.
They shall find real saints to draw from – Magdalene,
Peter, and Paul;
They shall work for an age at a sitting and never
be tired at all!

And only The Master shall praise us, and only
The Master shall blame;
And no one shall work for money, and no one shall
work for fame,
But each for the joy of the working, and each, in
his separate star,
Shall draw the Thing as he sees It for the God of Things
as They are!

The Holy War, 1917

('For here lay the excellent wisdom of him that built Mansoul, that the walls could never be broken down nor hurt by the most mighty adverse potentate unless the townsmen gave consent thereto.' – BUNYAN'S Holy War.)

A TINKER out of Bedford,
A vagrant oft in quod,
A private under Fairfax,
A minister of God –
Two hundred years and thirty
Ere Armageddon came
His single hand portrayed it,
And Bunyan was his name

He mapped for those who follow,
The world in which we are –
'This famous town of Mansoul'
That takes the Holy War,
Her true and traitor people,
The Gates along her wall,
From Eye Gate unto Feel Gate,
John Bunyan showed them all.

All enemy divisions,
Recruits of every class,
And highly screened positions
For flame or poison-gas;
The craft that we call modern,
The crimes that we call new,
John Bunyan had 'em typed and filed
In Sixteen Eighty-two.

DC
IV
DC

Likewise the Lords of Looseness
That hamper faith and works,
The Perseverance-Doubters,
And Present-Comfort shirks,
With brittle intellectuals
Who crack beneath a strain –
John Bunyan met that helpful set
In Charles the Second's reign

Emmanuel's vanguard dying
For right and not for rights,
My Lord Apollyon lying
To the State-kept Stockholmites,
The Pope, the swithering Neutrals,
The Kaiser and his Gott –
Their rôles, their goals, their naked souls –
He knew and drew the lot.

Now he hath left his quarters,
In Bunhill Fields to lie,
The wisdom that he taught us
Is proven prophecy –
One watchword through our Armies,
One answer form our Lands: –
'No dealings with Diabolus
As long as Mansoul stands!'

A pedlar from a hovel,
The lowest of the low –
The Father of the Novel,
Salvation's first Defoe –
Eight blinded generations
Ere Armageddon came,
He showed us how to meet it,
And Bunyan was his name!

McAndrew's Hymn, 1893

EXTRACT

LORD, THOU hast made this world below the
shadow of a dream,
An', taught by time, I tak' it so –
exceptin' always Steam.
From coupler-flange to spindle-guide
I see Thy Hand, O God –
Predestination in the stride
o' yon connectin'-rod.
John Calvin might ha' forged the same –
enorrmous, certain, slow –
Ay, wrought it in the furnace-flame –
my 'Institutio.'
I cannot get my sleep to-night;
old bones are hard to please;
I'll stand the middle watch up here –
alone wi' God an' these
My engines, after ninety days
o' race an' rack an' strain
Through all the seas of all Thy world,
slam-bangin' home again.
Slam-bang too much – they knock a wee –
the crosshead-gibs are loose,
But thirty thousand mile o' sea
has gied them fair excuse. . . .
Fine, clear an' dark – a full-draught breeze,
wi' Ushant out o' sight,
An' Ferguson relievin' Hay.
Old girl, ye'll walk to-night!
His wife's at Plymouth. . . . Seventy – One –
Two – Three since he began –
Three turns for Mistress Ferguson…
and who's to blame the man?

There's none at any port for me,
by drivin' fast or slow,
Since Elsie Campbell went to Thee,
Lord, thirty years ago

(The year the Sarah Sands was burned.
Oh, roads we used to tread,
Fra' Maryhill to Pollokshaws – fra'
Govan to Parkhead!)
Not but they're ceevil on the Board.
Ye'll hear Sir Kenneth say:
'Good morrn, McAndrew! Back again?
An' how's your bilge to-day?'
Miscallin' technicalities
but handin' me my chair
To drink Madeira wi' three Earls –
the auld Fleet Engineer
That started as a boiler-whelp –
when steam and he were low.
I mind the time we used to serve
a broken pipe wi' tow!
Ten pound was all the pressure then –
Eh! Eh! – a man wad drive;
An' here, our workin' gauges give
one hunder sixty-five!
We're creepin' on wi' each new rig –
less weight an' larger power;
There'll be there the loco-boiler next
an' thirty mile an hour!
Thirty an' more. What I ha' seen
since ocean-steam began
Leaves me na doot for the machine:
but what about the man?
The man that counts, wi' all his runs,
one million mile o' sea:
Four time the span from earth to moon...
How far, O Lord, from Thee

That wast beside him night an' day?
Ye mind my first typhoon?
It scoughed the skipper on his way
to jock wi' the saloon.
Three feet were on the stokehold-floor –
just slappin' to an' fro –
An' cast me on a furnace-door.
I have the marks to show.
Marks! I ha' marks o' more than burns –
deep in my soul an' black,
An' times like this, when things go smooth,
my wickudness comes back.
The sins o' four an' forty years,
all up an' down the seas,
Clack an' repeat like valves half-fed …
Forgie's our trespasses!
Nights when I'd come on deck to mark,
wi' envy in my gaze,
The couples kittlin' in the dark
between the funnel-stays;
Years when I raked the Ports wi' pride
to fill my cup o' wrong –
Judge not, O Lord, my steps aside
at Gay Street in Hong-Kong!
Blot out the wastrel hours of mine
in sin when I abode –
Jane Harrigan's an' Number Nine,
The Reddick an' Grant Road!
An' waur than all – my crownin' sin –
rank blasphemy an' wild.
I was not four and twenty then –
Ye wadna judge a child?
I'd seen the Tropics first that run –
new fruit, new smells, new air –
How could I tell – blind-fou wi' sun –
the Deil was lurkin' there?

By day like playhouse-scenes the shore
slid past our sleepy eyes;
By night those soft, lasceevious stars
leered from those velvet skies,
In port (we used no cargo-steam)
I'd daunder down the streets –
An ijjit grinnin' in a dream –
for shells an' parrakeets,
An walkin'-sticks o' carved bamboo
an' blowfish stuffed an' dried –
Fillin' my bunk wi' rubbishry
the Chief put overside.
Till, off Sambawa Head, Ye mind,
I heard a land-breeze ca',
Milk-warm wi' breath o' spice an' bloom:
'McAndrew, come awa'!'
Firm, clear an' low – no haste, no hate –
the ghostly whisper went,
Just statin' eevidential facts
beyon' all argument:
'Your mither's God's a graspin' deil,
the shadow o' yoursel',
'Got out o' books by meenisters
clean daft on Heaven an' Hell.
'They mak' him in thc Broomielaw,
o' Glasgie cold an' dirt,
'A jealous, pridefu' fetich, lad,
that's only strong to hurt.
'Ye'll not go back to Him again
an' kiss His red-hot rod,
'But come wi' Us' (Now, who were They?)
'an' know the Leevin' God,
'That does not kipper souls for sport
or break a life in jest,
'But swells the ripenin' cocoanuts
an' ripes the woman's breast.'

An' there it stopped – cut off – no more –
that quiet, certain voice –
For me, six months o' twenty-four,
to leave or take at choice.
'Twas on me like a thunderclap –
it racked me through an' through –
Temptation past the show o' speech,
unnameable an' new –
The Sin against the Holy Ghost?...
An' under all, our screw.

That storm blew by but left behind
her anchor-shiftin' swell.
Thou knowest all my heart an' mind.
Thou knowest, Lord, I fell –
Third on the Mary Gloster then,
and first that night in Hell!
Yet was Thy Hand beneath my head,
about my feet Thy Care –
Fra' Deli clear to Torres Strai,
the trail o' despair,

But when we touched the Barrier Reef
Thy answer to my prayer!...
We dared na run that sea by night
but lay an' held our fire,
An' I was drowsin' on the hatch –
sick – sick wi' doubt an' tire:
'Better the sight of eyes that see
than wanderin' o' desire!'
Ye mind that word? Clear as our gongs –
again, an' once again,
When rippin' down through coral-trash
ran out our moorin' chain:
An', by Thy Grace, I had the Light
to see my duty plain.
Light on the engine-room – no more –
bright as our carbons burn.
I've lost it since a thousand times,
but never past return!

Gethsemane—1914-18

THE GARDEN called Gethsemane
In Picardy it was,
And there the people came to see
The English soldiers pass.
We used to pass – we used to pass
Or halt, as it might be.
And ship our masks in case of gas
Beyond Gethsemane.

The Garden called Gethsemane
It held a pretty lass,
But all the time she talked to me
I prayed my cup might pass.
The officer sat on the chair,
The men lay on the grass,
And all the time we halted there
I prayed my cup might pass.

It didn't pass – it didn't pass –
It didn't pass from me.
I drank it when we met the gas
Beyond Gethsemane!

Mesopotamia, 1917

THEY SHALL not return to us, the resolute, the young,
The eager and whole-hearted whom we gave:
But the men who left them thriftily to die in their own dung,
Shall they come with years and honour to the grave?

They shall not return to us, the strong men coldly slain
In sight of help denied from day to day:
But the men who edged their agonies
and chid them in their pain,
Are they too strong and wise to put away?

Our dead shall not return to us while Day and Night divide –
Never while the bars of sunset hold.
But the idle-minded overlings who quibbled while they died,
Shall they thrust for high employments as of old?

Shall we only threaten and be angry for an hour?
When the storm is ended shall we find
How softly but how swiftly they have sidled back to power
By the favour and contrivance of their kind?

Even while they soothe us, while they promise large amends,
Even while they make a show of fear,
Do they call upon their debtors, and take counsel
with their friends,
To confirm and re-establish each career?

Their lives cannot repay us – their death could not undo –
The shame that they have laid upon our race.
But the slothfulness that wasted and the arrogance that slew,
Shall we leave it unabated in its place?

The Last Rhyme of True Thomas, 1893

EXTRACT

THE KING has called for priest and cup,
The King has taken spur and blade
To dub True Thomas a belted knight,
And all for the sake of the songs he made.

They have sought him high, they have sought him low,
They have sought him over down and lea.
They have found him by the milk-white thorn
That guards the Gates of Faerie.

'Twas bent beneath and blue above:
Their eyes were held that they might not see
The kine that grazed beneath the knowes,
Oh, they were the Queens of Faerie!

'Now cease your song,' the King he said,
'Oh, cease your song and get you dight
'To vow your vow and watch your arms,
'For I will dub you a belted knight.

'For I will give you a horse o' pride,
'Wi' blazon and spur and page and squire;
'Wi' keep and tail and seizin and law,
'And land to hold at your desire.'

True Thomas smiled above his harp,
And turned his face to the naked sky,
Where, blown before the wastrel wind,
The thistle-down she floated by.

'I ha' vowed my vow in another place,
'And bitter oath it was on me.
'I ha' watched my arms the lee-long night,
Where five-score fighting men would flee.

'My lance is tipped o' the hammered flame,
'My shield is beat o' the moonlight cold;
'And I won my spurs in the Middle World,
'A thousand fathom beneath the mould.

'And what should I make wi' a horse o' pride,
'And what should I make wi' a sword so brown,
'But spill the rings of the Gentle Folk
'And flyte my kin in the Fairy Town?

'And what should I make wi' blazon and belt,
'Wi' keep and tail and seizin and fee,
'And what should I do wi' page and squire
'That am a king in my own countrie?

'For I send east and I send west,
'And I send far as my will may flee,
'By dawn and dusk and the drinking rain,
'And syne my Sendings return to me.

'They come wi' news of the groanin' earth,
'They come wi' news of the roarin' sea.
'Wi' word of Spirit and Ghost and Flesh,
'And man, that's mazed among the three.'

Sussex, 1902

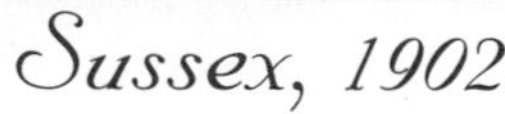

GOD GAVE all men all earth to love,
But since our hearts are small,
Ordained for each one spot should prove
Belovèd over all;
That, as He watched Creation's birth,
So we, in godlike mood,
May of our love create our earth
And see that it is good.

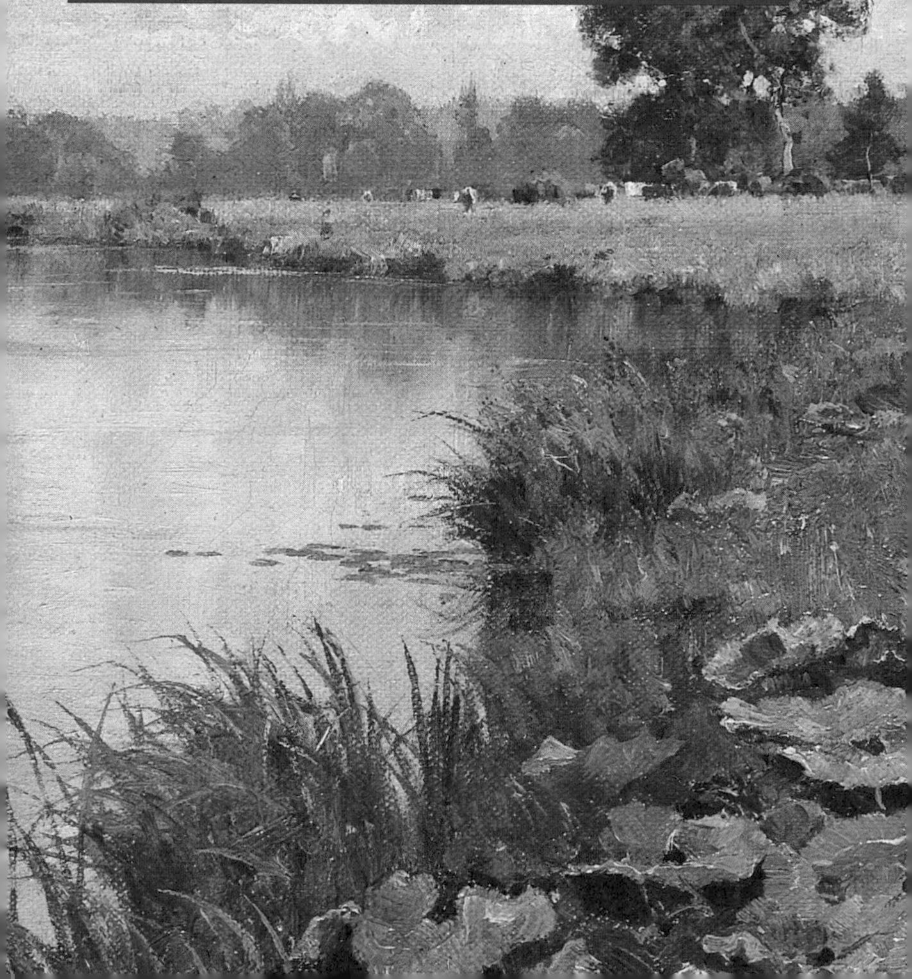

So one shall Baltic pines content,
As one some Surrey glade,
Or one the palm-grove's droned lament
Before Levuka's Trade.
Each to his choice, and I rejoice
The lot has fallen to me
In a fair ground – in a fair ground –
Yea, Sussex by the sea!

No tender-hearted garden crowns,
No bosomed woods adorn
Our blunt, bow-headed, whale-backed Downs,
But gnarled and writhen thorn –
Bare slopes where chasing shadows skim,
And, through the gaps revealed,
Belt upon belt, the wooded, dim,
Blue goodness of the Weald.

Clean of officious fence or hedge,
Half-wild and wholly tame,
The wise turf cloaks the white cliff-edge
As when the Romans came.
What sign of those that fought and died
At shift of sword and sword?
The barrow and the camp abide,
The sunlight and the sward.

Here leaps ashore the full Sou'west
All heavy-winged with brine,
Here lies above the folded crest
The Channel's leaden line;
And here the sea-fogs lap and cling,
And here, each warning each,
The sheep-bells and the ship-bells ring
Along the hidden beach.

We have no waters to delight
Our broad and brookless vales –
Only the dewpond on the height
Unfed, that never fails –
Whereby no tattered herbage tells
Which way the season flies –
Only our close-bit thyme that smells
Like dawn in Paradise.

Here through the strong and shadeless days
The tinkling silence thrills;
Or little, lost, Down churches praise
The Lord who made the hills:
But here the Old Gods guard their round,
And, in her secret heart,
The heathen kingdom Wilfrid found
Dreams, as she dwells, apart.

Though all the rest were all my share,
With equal soul I'd see
Her nine-and-thirty sisters fair,
Yet none more fair than she.
Choose ye your need from Thames to Tweed,
And I will choose instead
Such lands as lie 'twixt Rake and Rye,
Black Down and Beachy Head.

I will go out against the sun
Where the rolled scarp retires,
And the Long Man of Wilmington
Looks naked towards the shires;
And east till doubling Rother crawls
To find the fickle tide,
By dry and sea-forgotten walls,
Our ports of stranded pride.

I will go north about the shaws
And the deep ghylls that breed
Huge oaks and old, the which we hold
No more than Sussex weed;
Or south where windy Piddinghoe's
Begilded dolphin veers,
And red beside wide-bankèd Ouse
Lie down our Sussex steers.

So to the land our hearts we give
Till the sure magic strike,
And Memory, Use and Love make live
Us and our fields alike –
That deeper than our speech and thought,
Beyond our reason's sway,
Clay of the pit whence we were wrought
Yearns to its fellow-clay.

God gives all men all earth to love,
But, since man's heart is small,
Ordains for each one spot shall prove
Belovèd over all.
Each to his choice, and I rejoice
The lot has fallen to me
In a fair ground – in a fair ground –
Yea, Sussex by the sea!

The Sons of Martha, 1907

EXTRACT

THE SONS of Mary seldom bother, for they have
inherited that good part;
But the Sons of Martha favour their Mother of the
careful soul and the troubled heart.
And because she lost her temper once, and because
she was rude to the Lord her Guest,
Her Sons must wait upon Mary's Sons, world
without end, reprieve, or rest.

It is their care in all the ages to take the buffet
and cushion the shock.
It is their care that the gear engages; it is their
care that the switches lock.
It is their care that the wheels run truly; it is
their care to embark and entrain,
Tally, transport, and deliver duly the Sons of Mary
by land and main.

They say to mountains, 'Be ye removèd.' They say
to the lesser floods, 'Be dry.'
Under their rods are the rocks reprovèd – they are
not afraid of that which is high.
Then do the hill-tops shake to the summit – then is
the bed of the deep laid bare,
That the Sons of Mary may overcome it,
pleasantly sleeping and unaware.

They finger death at their gloves' end where they
piece and repiece the living wires.
He rears against the gates they tend: they feed
him hungry behind their fires.
Early at dawn, ere men see clear, they stumble
into his terrible stall,
And hale him forth like a haltered steer, and
goad and turn him till evenfall.

To these from birth is Belief forbidden; from these
till death is Relief afar.
They are concerned with matters hidden – under
the earth-line their altars are –
The secret fountains to follow up, waters
withdrawn to restore to the mouth,
And gather the floods as in a cup, and pour them
again at a city's drouth.

They do not preach that their God will rouse them
a little before the nuts work loose.
They do not teach that His Pity allows them to drop
their job when they dam'-well choose.
As in the thronged and the lighted ways, so in
the dark and the desert they stand,
Wary and watchful all their days that their brethren's
days may be long in the land.

Raise ye the stone or cleave the wood to make
a path more fair or flat –
Lo, it is black already with blood some Son of
Martha spilled for that!
Not as a ladder from earth to Heaven, not as a
witness to any creed,
But simple service simply given to his own kind
in their common need.

And the Sons of Mary smile and are blessèd – they
know the Angels are on their side.
They know in them is the Grace confessèd, and
for them are the Mercies multiplied.
They sit at the Feet – they hear the Word – they
see how truly the Promise runs.
They have cast their burden upon the Lord, and – the
Lord He lays it on Martha's Sons!

'For All We Have and Are'
1914

FOR ALL we have and are,
For all our children's fate,
Stand up and take the war.
The Hun is at the gate!
Our world has passed away,
In wantonness o'erthrown.
There is nothing left to-day
But steel and fire and stone!
Though all we knew depart,
The old Commandments stand: –
'In courage keep your heart,
In strength lift up your hand.'

Once more we hear the word
That sickened earth of old: –
'No law except the Sword
Unsheathed and uncontrolled.'
Once more it knits mankind,
Once more the nations go
To meet and break and bind
A crazed and driven foe.

Comfort, content, delight,
The ages' slow-bought gain,
They shrivelled in a night.
Only ourselves remain
To face the naked days
In silent fortitude,
Through perils and dismays
Renewed and re-renewed.
Though all we made depart,
The old Commandments stand: –
'In patience keep your heart,
In strength lift up your hand.'

No easy hope or lies
Shall bring us to our goal,
But iron sacrifice
Of body, will, and soul.
There is but one task for all –
One life for each to give.
What stands if Freedom fall?
Who dies if England live?

A Song in Storm, 1914-18

BE WELL assured that on our side
The abiding oceans fight,
Though headlong wind and heaping tide
Make us their sport to-night.
By force of weather, not of war,
In jeopardy we steer:
Then welcome Fate's discourtesy
Whereby it shall appear
How in all time of our distress,
And our deliverance too,
The game is more than the player of the game,
And the ship is more than the crew!

Out of the mist into the mirk
The glimmering combers roll.
Almost these mindless waters work
As though they had a soul –
Almost as though they leagued to whelm
Our flag beneath their green:
Then welcome Fate's discourtesy
Whereby it shall be seen, etc.

Be well assured, though wave and wind
Have mightier blows in store,
That we who keep the watch assigned
Must stand to it the more;
And as our streaming bows rebuke
Each billow's baulked career,
Sing, welcome Fate's discourtesy
Whereby it is made clear, etc.

No matter though our decks be swept
And mast and timber crack –
We can make good all loss except
The loss of turning back.
So, 'twixt these Devils and our deep
Let courteous trumpets sound,
To welcome Fate's discourtesy
Whereby it will be found, etc.

Be well assured, though in our power
Is nothing left to give
But chance and place to meet the hour,
And leave to strive to live,
Till these dissolve our Order holds,
Our Service binds us here.
Then welcome Fate's discourtesy
Whereby it is made clear
How in all time of our distress,
As in our triumph too,
The game is more than the player of the game,
And the ship is more than the crew!

The Gipsy Trail

THE WHITE moth to the closing bine,
The bee to the opened clover,
And the gipsy blood to the gipsy blood
Ever the wide world over.

Ever the wide world over, lass,
Ever the trail held true,
Over the world and under the world,
And back at the last to you.

Out of the dark of the gorgio camp,
Out of the grime and the gray
(Morning waits at the end of the world),
Gipsy, come away!

The wild boar to the sun-dried swamp,
The red crane to her reed,
And the Romany lass to the Romany lad
By the tie of a roving breed.

The pied snake to the rifted rock,
The buck to the stony plain,
And the Romany lass to the Romany lad,
And both to the road again.

Both to the road again, again!
Out on a clean sea-track –
Follow the cross of the gipsy trail
Over the world and back!

Follow the Romany patteran
North where the blue bergs sail
And the bows are gray with the frozen spray,
And the masts are shod with mail.

Follow the Romany patteran
Sheer to the Austral Light,
Where the besom of God is the wild South wind,
Sweeping the sea-floors white.

Follow the Romany patteran
West to the sinking sun,
Till the junk-sails lift through the houseless drift,
And the east and the west are one.

Follow the Romany patteran
East where the silence broods
By a purple wave on an opal beach
In the hush of the Mahim woods.

'The wild hawk to the wind-swept sky,
The deer to the wholesome wold,
And the heart of a man to the heart of a maid,
As it was in the days of old.'

The heart of a man to the heart of a maid –
Light of my tents, be fleet.
Morning waits at the end of the world,
And the world is all at our feet!

The Craftsman

ONCE, AFTER long-drawn revel at The Mermaid,
He to the overbearing Boanerges
Jonson, uttered (if half of it were liquor,
Blessed be the vintage!)

Saying how, at an alehouse under Cotswold,
He had made sure of his very Cleopatra
Drunk with enormous, salvation-contemning
Love for a tinker.

How, while he hid from Sir Thomas's keepers,
Crouched in a ditch and drenched by the midnight
Dews, he had listened to gipsy Juliet
Rail at the dawning.

How at Bankside, a boy drowning kittens
Winced at the business; whereupon his sister –
Lady Macbeth aged seven – thrust 'em under,
Sombrely scornful.

How on a Sabbath, hushed and compassionate –
She being known since her birth to the townsfolk –
Stratford dredged and delivered from Avon
Dripping Ophelia.

So, with a thin third finger marrying
Drop to wine-drop domed on the table,
Shakespeare opened his heart till the sunrise
Entered to hear him.

London waked and he, imperturbable,
Passed from waking to hurry after shadows …
Busied upon shows of no earthly importance?
Yes, but he knew it!

Shillin' a Day

MY NAME is O'Kelly, I've heard the Revelly
From Birr to Bareilly, from Leeds to Lahore,
Hong-Kong and Peshawur,
Lucknow and Etawah,
And fifty-five more all endin' in 'pore'.
Black Death and his quickness, the depth and the thickness
Of sorrow and sickness I've known on my way,
But I'm old and I'm nervis,
I'm cast from the Service
And all I deserve is a shillin' a day.
Shillin' a day,
Bloomin' good pay –
Lucky to touch it, a shillin' a day!

Oh, it drives me half crazy to think of the days I
Went slap for the Ghazi, my sword at my side,
When we rode Hell-for-leather
Both squadrons together,
That didn't care whether we lived or we died.
But it's no use despairin', my wife must go charin'
An' me commissairin', the pay-bills to better,
So if me you be'old
In the wet and the cold,
By the Grand Metropold, won't you give me a letter?

Give 'im a letter –
'Can't do no better,
Late Troop-Sergeant-Major an' – runs with a letter!
Think what 'e's been,
Think what 'e's seen.
Think of his pension an' –
GAWD SAVE THE QUEEN!

The Return

(ALL ARMS)

PEACE IS declared an' I return
To 'Ackneystadt, but not the same;
Things 'ave transpired which made me learn
The size and meanin' of the game.
I did no more than others did,
I don't know where the change began.
I started as a average kid,
I finished as a thinkin' man.

If England was what England seems,
An' not the England of our dreams,
But only putty, brass, an' paint,
'Ow quick we'd drop 'er! But she ain't!

Before my gappin' mouth could speak
I 'eard it in my comrade's tone.
I saw it on my neighbour's cheek
Before I felt it flush my own.
An' last it come to me – not pride,
Not yet conceit, but on the 'ole
(If such a term may be applied),
The makin's of a bloomin' soul.

Rivers at night that cluck an' jeer,
Plains which the moonshine turns to sea,
Mountains which never let you near,
An' stars to all eternity;
An' the quick-breathin' dark that fills
The 'ollows of the wilderness,
When the wind worries through the 'ills –
These may 'ave taught me more or less.

Towns without people, ten times took,
An' ten times left an' burned at last;
An' starving dogs that come to look
For owners when a column passed;
An' quiet, 'omesick talks between
Men, met by night, you never knew
Until – 'is face – by shellfire seen –
Once – an' struck off. They taught me too.

The day's lay-out – the mornin' sun
Beneath your 'at-brim as you sight;
The dinner-'ush from noon till one,
An' the full roar that lasts till night;
An' the pore dead that look so old
An' was so young an hour ago,
An' legs tied down before they're cold –
These are the things which make you know.

Also Time runnin' into years –
A thousand Places left be'ind –
An' Men from both two 'emispheres
Discussin' things of every kind;
So much more near than I 'ad known,
So much more great than I 'ad guessed –
An' me, like all the rest, alone –
But reachin' out to all the rest!

So 'ath it come to me – not pride,
Nor yet conceit, but on the 'ole
(If such a term may be applied),
The makin's of a bloomin' soul.
But now, discharged, I fall away
To do with little things again. . . .
Gawd, 'oo knows all I cannot say,
Look after me in Thamesfontein!

If England was what England seems,
An' not the England of our dreams,
But only putty, brass, an' paint,
'Ow quick we'd chuck 'er! But she ain't!

The Married Man

THE BACHELOR 'e fights for one
As joyful as can be;
But the married man don't call it fun,
Because 'e fights for three –
For 'Im an' 'Er an' It
(An' Two an' One make Three)
'E wants to finish 'is little bit,
An' 'e wants to go 'ome to 'is tea!

The bachelor pokes up 'is 'ead
To see if you are gone;
But the married man lies down instead,
An' waits till the sights come on,
For 'Im an' 'Er an' a hit
(Direct or ricochee)
'E wants to finish 'is little bit,
An' 'e wants to go 'ome to 'is tea.

The bachelor will miss you clear
To fight another day;
But the married man, 'e says 'No fear!'
'E wants you out of the way
Of 'Im an' 'Er an' It
(An' 'is road to 'is farm or the sea),
'E wants to finish 'is little bit,
An' 'e wants to go 'ome to 'is tea.

The bachelor 'e fights 'is fight
An' stretches out an' snores;
But the married man sits up all night –
For 'e don't like out-o'-doors.
'E'll strain an' listen an' peer
An' give the first alarm –
For the sake o' the breathin' 'e's used to 'ear,
An' the 'ead on the thick of 'is arm.

The bachelor may risk 'is 'ide
To 'elp you when you're downed;
But the married man will wait beside
Till the ambulance comes round.
'E'll take your 'ome address
An' all you've time to say,
Or if 'e sees there's 'ope, 'e'll press
Your art'ry 'alf the day –

For 'Im an' 'Er an' It
(An' One from Three leaves Two),
For 'e knows you wanted to finish your bit,
An' 'e knows 'oo's wantin' you.
Yes, 'Im an' 'Er an' It
(Our 'oly One in Three),
We're all of us anxious to finish our bit,
An' we want to get 'ome to our tea!

Yes, It an' 'Er an' 'Im,
Which often makes me think
The married man must sink or swim
An' – 'e can't afford to sink!
Oh, 'Im an' It an' 'Er
Since Adam an' Eve began!
So I'd rather fight with the bacheler
An' be nursed by the married man!

'Cities and Thrones and Powers'

('*A CENTURION OF THE THIRTIETH*' – PUCK OF POOK'S HILL)

CITIES AND Thrones and Powers
Stand in Time's eye,
Almost as long as flowers,
Which daily die:
But, as new buds put forth
To glad new men,
Out of the spent and unconsidered Earth
The Cities rise again.

This season's Daffodil,
She never hears
What change, what chance, what chill,
Cut down last year's;
But with bold countenance,
And knowledge small,
Esteems her seven days' continuance
To be perpetual.

So Time that is o'er-kind
To all that be,
Ordains us e'en as blind,
As bold as she:
That in our very death,
And burial sure,
Shadow to shadow, well persuaded, saith,
'See how our works endure!'

Puck's Song

ENLARGED FROM PUCK OF POOK'S HILL

SEE YOU the ferny ride that steals
Into the oak-woods far?
O that was whence they hewed the keels
That rolled to Trafalgar.

And mark you where the ivy clings
To Bayham's mouldering walls?
O there we cast the stout railings
That stand around St. Paul's.

See you the dimpled track that runs
All hollow through the wheat?
O that was where they hauled the guns
That smote King Philip's fleet.

(Out of the Weald, the secret Weald
Men sent in ancient years
The horse-shoes red at Flodden Field
The arrows at Poitiers!)

See you our little mill that clacks,
So busy by the brook?
She has ground her corn and paid her tax
Ever since Domesday Book.

See you our stilly woods of oak,
And the dread ditch beside?
O that was where the Saxons broke
On the day that Harold died.

See you the windy levels spread
About the gates of Rye?
O that was where the Northmen fled,
When Alfred's ships came by.

See you our pastures wide and lone,
Where the red oxen browse?
O there was a City thronged and known,
Ere London boasted a house.

And see you, after rain, the trace
Of mound and ditch and wall?
O that was a Legion's camping-place,
When Caesar sailed from Gaul.

And see you marks that show and fade,
Like shadows on the Downs?
O they are the lines the Flint Men made,
To guard their wondrous towns.

Trackway and Camp and City lost,
Salt Marsh where now is corn –
Old Wars, old Peace, old Arts that cease,
And so was England born!

She is not any common Earth,
Water or wood or air,
But Merlin's Isle of Gramarye
Where you and I will fare!

Sir Richard's Song (A. D. 1066)
('YOUNG MEN AT THE MANOR' – PUCK OF POOK'S HILL)

I FOLLOWED my Duke ere I was a lover,
To take from England fief and fee;
But now this game is the other way over –
But now England hath taken me!

I had my horse, my shield and banner,
And a boy's heart, so whole and free;
But now I sing in another manner –
But now England hath taken me!

As for my Father in his tower,
Asking news of my ship at sea,
He will remember his own hour –
Tell him England hath taken me!

As for my Mother in her bower,
That rules my Father so cunningly,
She will remember a maiden's power –
Tell her England hath taken me!

As for my Brother in Rouen City,
A nimble and naughty page is he,
But he will come to suffer and pity –
Tell him England hath taken me!

As for my little Sister waiting
In the pleasant orchards of Normandie,
Tell her youth is the time for mating –
Tell her England hath taken me!

As for my comrades in camp and highway,
That lift their eyebrows scornfully,
Tell them their way is not my way –
Tell them England hath taken me!

Kings and Princes and Barons famèd,
Knights and Captains in your degree;
Hear me a little before I am blamèd –
Seeing England hath taken me!

Howso great man's strength be reckoned,
There are two things he cannot flee.
Love is the first and Death is the second –
And Love in England hath taken me!

A Charm

(INTRODUCTION TO *REWARDS AND FAIRIES*)

TAKE OF English earth as much
As either hand may rightly clutch.
In the taking of it breathe
Prayer for all who lie beneath.
Not the great or well-bespoke,
But the mere uncounted folk
Of whose life and death is none
Report or lamentation.
Lay that earth upon thy heart,
And thy sickness shall depart!

It shall sweeten and make whole
Fevered breath and festered soul.
It shall mightily restrain
Over-busied hand and brain.
It shall ease thy mortal strife
'Gainst the immortal woe of life,
Till thyself, restored, shall prove
By what grace the Heavens do move.

Take of English flowers these –
Spring's full-facèd primroses,
Summer's wild wide-hearted rose,
Autumn's wall-flower of the close,
And, thy darkness to illume,
Winter's bee-thronged ivy-bloom.
Seek and serve them where they bide
From Candlemas to Christmas-tide,
For these simples, used aright,
Can restore a failing sight.

These shall cleanse and purify
Webbed and inward-turning eye;
These shall show thee treasure hid
Thy familiar fields amid;
And reveal (which is thy need)
Every man a King indeed!

Cold Iron

('COLD IRON' – *REWARDS AND FAIRIES*)

'GOLD IS for the mistress – silver for the maid –
Copper for the craftsman cunning at his trade.'
'Good!' said the Baron, sitting in his hall,
'But Iron – Cold Iron – is master of them all.'

So he made rebellion 'gainst the King his liege,
Camped before his citadel and summoned it to siege.
'Nay!' said the cannoneer on the castle wall,
'But Iron – Cold Iron – shall be master of you all!'

Woe for the Baron and his knights so strong,
When the cruel cannon-balls laid 'em all along;
He was taken prisoner, he was cast in thrall,
And Iron – Cold Iron – was master of it all!

Yet his King spake kindly (ah, how kind a Lord!)
'What if I release thee now and give thee back thy sword?'
'Nay!' said the Baron, 'mock not at my fall,
For Iron – Cold Iron – is master of men all.'

'Tears are for the craven, prayers are for the clown –
Halters for the silly neck that cannot keep a crown.'
'As my loss is grievous, so my hope is small,
For Iron – Cold Iron – must be master of men all!'

Yet his King made answer (few such Kings there be!)
'Here is bread and here is Wine – sit and sup with me.
Eat and drink in Mary's Name, the whiles I do recall
How Iron – Cold Iron – can be master of men all!'

He took the Wine and blessed it. He blessed and
break the Bread.
With His own Hands He served Them, and presently
He said:
'See! These Hands they pierced with nails, outside
My city wall,
Show Iron – Cold Iron – to be master of
men all.

'Wounds are for the desperate, blows are for
the strong.
Balm and oil for weary hearts all cut and bruised
with wrong.
I forgive thy treason – I redeem
thy fall –
For Iron – Cold Iron – must be master
of men all!'

'Crowns are for the valiant – sceptres for the bold!
Thrones and powers for mighty men who dare to
take and hold!'
'Nay!' said the Baron, kneeling in his hall,
'But Iron – Cold Iron – is master of men all!
Iron out of Calvary is master of men all!'

A Pict Song

('THE WINGED HATS' – PUCK OF POOK'S HILL)

ROME NEVER looks where she treads.
Always her heavy hooves fall
On our stomachs, our hearts or our heads;
And Rome never heeds when we bawl.
Her sentries pass on – that is all,
And we gather behind them in hordes,
And plot to reconquer the Wall,
With only our tongues for our swords.

We are the Little Folk – we!
Too little to love or to hate.
Leave us alone and you'll see
How we can drag down the State!
We are the worm in the wood!
We are the rot at the root!
We are the taint in the blood!
We are the thorn in the foot!

Mistletoe killing an oak –
Rats gnawing cables in two –
Moths making holes in a cloak –
How they must love what they do!
Yes – and we Little Folk too,
We are busy as they –
Working our works out of view –
Watch, and you'll see it some day!

No indeed! We are not strong,
But we know Peoples that are.
Yes, and we'll guide them along
To smash and destroy you in War

We shall be slaves just the same?
Yes, we have always been slaves
But you – you will die of the shame,
And then we shall dance on your graves!

We are the Little Folk, we, etc.

The Law of the Jungle

('HOW FEAR CAME' – THE SECOND JUNGLE BOOK)

NOW THIS is the Law of the Jungle – as old and as true
as the sky;
And the Wolf that shall keep it may prosper, but the
Wolf that shall break it must die.

As the creeper that girdles the tree-trunk the Law
runneth forward and back –
For the strength of the Pack is the Wolf, and the
strength of the Wolf is the Pack.

Wash daily from nose-tip to tail-tip; drink deeply,
but never too deep;
And remember the night is for hunting, and forget
not the day is for sleep.

The Jackal may follow the Tiger, but, Cub, when
thy whiskers are grown,
Remember the Wolf is a hunter – go forth and
get food of thine own.

Keep peace with the Lords of the Jungle – the
Tiger, the Panther, the Bear;
And trouble not Hathi the Silent, and mock not
the Boar in his lair.

When Pack meets with Pack in the Jungle, and
neither will go from the trail,
Lie down till the leaders have spoken – it may
be fair words shall prevail.

When ye fight with a Wolf of the Pack, ye must
fight him alone and afar,
Lest others take part in the quarrel, and the
Pack be diminished by war.

The Lair of the Wolf is his refuge, and where he
has made him his home,
Not even the Head Wolf may enter, not even
the Council may come.

The Lair of the Wolf is his refuge, but where he
has digged it too plain,
The Council shall send him a message, and so
he shall change it again.

If ye kill before midnight, be silent, and wake
not the woods with your bay,
Lest ye frighten the deer from the crops, and
the brothers go empty away.

Ye may kill for yourselves, and your mates,
and your cubs as they need, and ye can;
But kill not for pleasure of killing, and *seven
times never kill Man!*

If ye plunder his Kill from a weaker, devour
not all in thy pride;
Pack-Right is the right of the meanest; so leave
him the head and the hide.

The Kill of the Pack is the meat of the Pack. Ye
must eat where it lies;
And no one may carry away of that meat to
his lair, or he dies.

The Kill of the Wolf is the meat of the Wolf. He
may do what he will,
But, till he has given permission, the Pack may
not eat of that Kill.

Cub-Right is the right of the Yearling. From all
of his Pack he may claim
Full-gorge when the killer has eaten; and none
may refuse him the same.

Lair-Right is the right of the Mother. From all of
her year she may claim
One haunch of each kill for her litter; and none
may deny her the same.

Cave-Right is the right of the Father – to hunt
by himself for his own:
He is freed of all calls to the Pack; he is judged
by the Council alone.

Because of his age and his cunning, because of
his gripe and his paw,
In all that the Law leaveth open, the word of
the Head Wolf is Law.

Now these are the Laws of the Jungle, and
many and mighty are they;
But the head and the hoof of the Law and the
haunch and the hump is – Obey!

The Children's Song
(PUCK OF POOK'S HILL)

LAND OF our Birth, we pledge to thee
Our love and toil in the years to be;
When we are grown and take our place
As men and women with our race.

Father in Heaven who lovest all,
Oh, help Thy children when they call;
That they may build from age to age
An undefilèd heritage.

Teach us to bear the yoke in youth,
With steadfastness and careful truth;
That, in our time, Thy Grace may give
The Truth whereby the Nations live.

Teach us to rule ourselves alway,
Controlled and cleanly night and day;
That we may bring, if need arise,
No maimed or worthless sacrifice.

Teach us to look in all our ends
On Thee for judge, and not our friends;
That we, with Thee, may walk uncowed
By fear or favour of the crowd.

Teach us the Strength that cannot seek,
By deed or thought, to hurt the weak;
That, under Thee, we may possess
Man's strength to comfort man's distress.

Teach us Delight in simple things,
And Mirth that has no bitter springs;
Forgiveness free of evil done,
And Love to all men 'neath the Sun!

Land of our Birth, our faith, our pride,
For whose dear sake our fathers died;
Oh, Motherland, we pledge to thee
Head, heart and hand through the years to be!

If –

('BROTHER SQUARE-TOES' – *REWARDS AND FAIRIES*)

IF YOU can keep your head when all about you
Are losing theirs and blaming it on you,
If you can trust yourself when all men doubt you.
But make allowance for their doubting too;
If you can wait and not be tired by waiting,
Or being lied about, don't deal in lies,
Or being hated, don't give way to hating,
And yet don't look too good, nor talk too wise:

If you can dream – and not make dreams your master
If you can think – and not make thoughts your aim
If you can meet with Triumph and Disaster
And treat those two impostors just the same;
If you can bear to hear the truth you've spoken
Twisted by knaves to make a trap for fools.
Or watch the things you gave your life to, broken,
And stoop and build 'em up with worn-out tools:

If you can make one heap of all your winnings
And risk it on one turn of pitch-and-toss,
And lose, and start again at your beginnings
And never breathe a word about your loss;
If you can force your heart and nerve and sinew
To serve your turn long after they are gone,
And so hold on when there is nothing in you
Except the Will which says to them: 'Hold on!'

If you can talk with crowds and keep your virtue,
Or walk with Kings – nor lose the common touch,
If neither foes nor loving friends can hurt you,
If all men count with you, but none too much;
If you can fill the unforgiving minute
With sixty seconds' worth of distance run,
Yours is the Earth and everything that's in it,
And – which is more – you'll be a Man, my son!

The Queen's Men

('GLORIANA' – *REWARDS AND FAIRIES*)

VALOUR AND Innocence
Have latterly gone hence
To certain death by certain shame attended.
Envy – ah! even to tears! –
The fortune of their years
Which, though so few, yet so divinely ended.

Scarce had they lifted up
Life's full and fiery cup,
Than they had set it down untouched before them.
Before their day arose
They beckoned it to close –
Close in confusion and destruction o'er them.

They did not stay to ask
What prize should crown their task –
Well sure that prize was such as no man strives for;
But passed into eclipse
Her kiss upon their lips –
Even Belphœbe's, whom they gave their lives for!

Mowgli's Song Against People
('LETTING IN THE JUNGLE' – THE SECOND JUNGLE BOOK)

I WILL let loose against you the fleet-footed vines –
I will call in the Jungle to stamp out your lines!
The roofs shall fade before it,
The house-beams shall fall;
And the *Karela*, the bitter *Karela*,
Shall cover it all!

In the gates of these your councils my people shall sing.
In the doors of these your garners the Bat-folk shall cling;
And the snake shall be your watchman,
By a hearthstone unswept;
For the *Karela*, the bitter *Karela*,
Shall fruit where ye slept!

Ye shall not see my strikers; ye shall hear them and guess.
By night, before the moon-rise, I will send for my cess,
And the wolf shall be your herdsman
By a landmark removed;
For the *Karela*, the bitter *Karela*,
Shall seed where ye loved!

I will reap your fields before you at the hands of a host.
Ye shall glean behind my reapers for the bread that is lost;
And the deer shall be your oxen
On a headland untilled;
For the *Karela*, the bitter *Karela*,
Shall leaf where ye build!

I have untied against you the club-footed vines –
I have sent in the Jungle to swamp out your lines!
The trees – the trees are on you!
The house-beams shall fall;
And the *Karela*, the bitter *Karela*,
Shall cover you all!

The Roman Centurion's Song

(ROMAN OCCUPATION OF BRITAIN, A.D. 300)

LEGATE, I had the news last night – my cohort ordered home
By ship to Portus Itius and thence by road to Rome
I've marched the companies aboard, the arms are stowed below:
Now let another take my sword. Command me not to go!

I've served in Britain forty years, from Vectis to the Wall.
I have none other home than this, nor any life at all.
Last night I did not understand, but, now the hour draws near
That calls me to my native land, I feel that land is here.

Here where men say my name was made, here where my work was done;
Here where my dearest dead are laid – my wife – my wife and son;
Here where time, custom, grief and toil, age, memory, service, love,
Have rooted me in British soil. Ah, how can I remove?

For me this land, that sea, these airs, those folk and fields suffice.
What purple Southern pomp can match our changeful Northern skies,
Black with December snows unshed or pearled with August haze –
The clanging arch of steel-grey March, or June's long-lighted days?

You'll follow widening Rhodanus till vine and olive lean
Aslant before the sunny breeze that sweeps Nemausus clean
To Arelate's triple gate; but let me linger on,
Here where our stiff-necked British oaks confront Euroclydon!
You'll take the old Aurelian Road through shore-descending pines
Where, blue as any peacock's neck, the Tyrrhene Ocean shines.
You'll go where laurel crowns are won, but – will you e'er forget.
The scent of hawthorn in the sun, or bracken in the wet?

Let me work here for Britain's sake – at any task you will –
A marsh to drain, a road to make or native troops to drill.
Some Western camp (I know the Pict) or granite Border keep,
Mid seas of heather derelict, where our old messmates sleep.

Legate, I come to you in tears – My cohort
ordered home!
I've served in Britain forty years. What should I do
in Rome?
Here is my heart, my soul, my mind – the only life
I know.
I cannot leave it all behind. Command me
not to go!

Gertrude's Prayer
('DAYSPRING MISHANDLED')

THAT WHICH is marred at birth Time shall not mend,
Nor water out of bitter well make clean;
All evil thing returneth at the end,
Or elseway walketh in our blood unseen.
Whereby the more is sorrow in certaine –
Dayspring mishandled cometh not againe.

To-bruizèd be that slender, sterting spray
Out of oake's rind that should betide
A branch of girt and goodliness, straightway
Her spring is turnèd on herself, and wried
And knotted like some gall or veiney wen. –
Dayspring mishandled cometh not agen.

Noontide repayeth never morning-bliss –
Sith noon to morn is incomparable;
And, so it be our dawning goth amiss,
None other after-hour serveth well.
Ah! Jesu-Moder, pitie my oe paine –
Dayspring mishandled cometh not againe!

The Appeal

IF I have given you delight
By aught that I have done,
Let me lie quiet in that night
Which shall be yours anon:

And for the little, little, span
The dead are borne in mind,
Seek not to question other than
The books I leave behind.

Index to First Lines

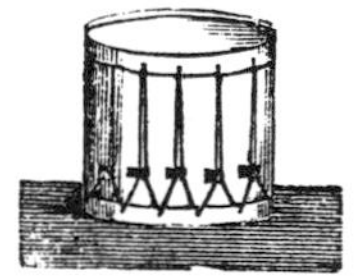

Notes on Illustrations

3 *Rudyard Kipling,* by P. Burn Jones (National Portrait Gallery, London).Courtesy of Visual Arts Library.

5 *Entrance to Sardar Market,* by Penelope Anstice (Private Collection).Courtesy of The Bridgeman Art Library.

7 *Mr Rudyard Kipling takes a bloomin' day aht, on the blasted 'eath, along with Brittania, 'is gurl,* by Max Beerbohm (Central Saint Martin's College of Art and Design). Courtesy of The Bridgeman Art Library.

12 *Bateman's, Kipling's House,* Sussex. Courtesy of The Bridgeman Art Library.

15 *Benares,* by Albert Goodwin (Chris Beetles Ltd., London). Courtesy of The Bridgeman Art Library.

19 *Fourth Dragoon Guards Leaving for the Crimean War,* Anonymous (Private Collection). Courtesy of The Bridgeman Art Library.

23 *Eastward Ho!,* by Henry Nelson O'Neil (Forbes Magazine Collection, New York). Courtesy of The Bridgeman Art Library.

26-7 *Bombay,* by John Strickland Goodall (Christopher Wood Gallery, London). Courtesy of The Bridgeman Art Library.

29 *The Guards Cheer,* by Sir Hubert Von Herkomer (Christopher Wood Gallery, London). Courtesy of The Bridgeman Art Library.

30 *Jessie's Dream,* by Fredrick Goodall (Sheffield City Art Galleries). Courtesy of The Bridgeman Art Library.

34-5 *Late Summer on the River Mole, near Dorking,* by Edward Wilkins Waite (Private Collection). Courtesy of The Bridgeman Art Library.

41 *Pont de l'Europe,* by Claude Monet (Marmottan, Paris). Courtesy Visual Arts Library.

47 *Gypsies Camping by a Path,* by William West (Agnew & Sons). Courtesy of The Bridgeman Art Library.

50 *A blacksmith disputing the Price of Iron...,* by J.W.Turner (Tate Gallery, London). Courtesy of Visual Arts Library.

52-3 *Listed for the Connaught Rangers,* by Lady E. Southerden Thompson (Bury Art Gallery & Museum). Courtesy of The Bridgeman Art Library.

57 *A Father's Welcome,* by Frederick Morgan (Phillips, The International Fine Art Auctioneers). Courtesy of The Bridgeman Art Library.

61 *The Widow Whitgift & Her Sons,* by Arthur Rackham (Victoria & Albert Museum). Courtesy of The Bridgeman Art Library.

66 *The Downs at Midhurst,* by Henry Maplestone (Warrington Museum & Art Gallery, Cheshire). Courtesy of The Bridgeman Art Library.

68-9 *The Fort at Amber, Rajasthan,* by William Simpson (British Library, London). Courtesy of The Bridgeman Art Library.

72 *Oberon, Puck and Titania with Fairies Dancing,* by William Blake (Tate Gallery, London). Courtesy of The Bridgeman Art Library.

75 *Shere Khan in the Jungle,* by Detmold brothers (Private Collection).

78 *The Venturesome Robin,* by William Collins (Private Collection). Courtesy of Visual Arts Library.

81 *The Marble Rocks, Jabalpur,* by Edward Lear (Christie's London). Courtesy of The Bridgeman Art Library.

83 *Scotland Forever,* by Lady E. Southerden Thompson Butler (City Art Gallery, Leeds). Courtesy of The Bridgeman Art Library.

87 *Faithful unto Death,* by Sir Edward John Poynter (Forbex Magazine Collection, London). Courtesy of The Bridgeman Art Library.

91 *The Indian Jugglers,* by J. Green (The Fine Art Society, London). Courtesy of The Bridgeman Art Library.

95 *An Indian Funeral Procession,* by Albert Goodwin (Maidstone Museum and Art Gallery, Kent). Courtesy of The Bridgeman Art Library.